DO DINOSAURS FLY?
PREHISTORIC ANIMAL LEARNING FOR KIDS OF ALL AGES

BABY PROFESSOR

EDUCATION KIDS

The word dinosaur comes from the Greek language and means 'terrible lizard'.

Dinosaurs ruled the Earth for over 135 million years. They first appeared during the Triassic period, 231 million years ago.

It is believed that dinosaurs lived on Earth until around 65 million years ago when a mass extinction occurred.

All dinosaurs
laid eggs.
About 40
kinds of
dinosaur eggs
have been
discovered.

Meat-eating dinosaurs are known as theropods, which means beast-footed because they had sharp, hooked claws on their toes.

Dinosaurs lived on all the continents, including Antarctica.

Pterodactyls are not dinosaurs, they were flying reptiles that lived during the age of dinosaurs.

Scientists believe that the event leading to the extinction may have been a massive asteroid impact or huge volcanic activity.